VISION

The Life and Music of

Hildegard von Bingen

..

VISION

The Life and Music of
HILDEGARD
VON BINGEN

Compiled and Edited by

▪ *Jane Bobko* ▪

With Text by Barbara Newman
and Commentary by Matthew Fox

PENGUIN
STUDIO

PENGUIN STUDIO BOOKS
Published by the Penguin Group
Penguin Books USA Inc., 375 Hudson Street,
New York, New York 10014, U.S.A.
Penguin Books Ltd, 27 Wrights Lane, London W8 5TZ, England
Penguin Books Australia Ltd, Ringwood, Victoria, Australia
Penguin Books Canada Ltd, 10 Alcorn Avenue,
Toronto, Ontario, Canada M4V 3B2
Penguin Books (N.Z.) Ltd, 182–190 Wairau Road,
Auckland 10, New Zealand

Penguin Books Ltd, Registered Offices:
Harmondsworth, Middlesex, England

First published in 1995 by Viking Penguin,
a division of Penguin Books USA Inc.

3 5 7 9 10 8 6 4 2

Copyright © 1995 Penguin Books USA, Inc., 1995
All rights reserved

Pages 109 and 110 constitute an extension of this copyright page.

CIP data available
ISBN 0-670-86405-6

Cover art by Marvin Mattelson
Copyright © Angel Records

Printed in Tokyo
Set in Cloister
Designed by Francesca Belanger

CONTENTS

PREFACE

I n convents," said the great German writer Heinrich von Kleist, "the nuns, who are trained to play every kind of instrument, provide their own music, which is often of a precision, an understanding, and a depth of feeling that one misses in male orchestras (perhaps because of the feminine character of this mysterious art)." "Saint Cecilia, or the Power of Music," from which this passage comes, is the story of a miracle: four brothers, iconoclasts all, are restrained from the profanation of a convent church when, during a solemn Corpus Christi celebration, Saint Cecilia appears to conduct the music for the Mass. Kleist was describing Aachen, at the end of the sixteenth century. But his words might be applied equally to the Rupertsberg, in the latter half of the twelfth century. The Rupertsberg was the site of a cloister founded by Hildegard von Bingen, the composer of more than seventy religious songs and of a morality play set to music. Though no instruments, other than a discreet drone or conceivably an organ, were used in the performance of Hildegard's songs, her music had the power that Kleist ascribed to Saint Cecilia's Mass: it caused a revolution in the soul.

In Hildegard's life of intense creativity, her "feminine character," as Kleist would have called it, was not incidental. She was a visionary, and for women in the Middle Ages visions were a route to power—once it was acknowledged that God spoke through these visions, women were endowed with the authority to teach, to speak out, to act both within the Church and in the world, and to be an example to other women. Visions were also the road to art. In Hildegard's case, she shaped the stuff of her visions into books, and created music as a window onto mystical experience.

The compositions on Angel Records' *Vision* compact disc

present Hildegard's original twelfth-century lyrics, with arrangements and interpretations by Richard Souther that place contemporary musical elements underneath the vocals. With the exception of "Living Fountain," which is from Hildegard's musical drama *Ordo virtutum (Play of the Virtues)*, all of the selections come from her cycle *Symphonia armonie celestium revelationum (Symphony of the Harmony of Celestial Revelations)*. Two of the tracks, "The Living Light" and "The Anointing," are original instrumental compositions by Souther, which are intended to act, the composer has said, "as the word *selah* ('to pause and reflect') does in the Psalms. I wanted musically to create images that would take the listener to a reflective place. 'The Anointing' is, to me, musical images of the Book of Revelation. 'The Living Light' is an aural representation of the peace one receives in communion with God." The "desire to worship our Creator," the composer has indicated, is the impulse that marries Hildegard's original music to his own.

The performers and producers of *Vision* hoped to rouse the listener to learn more about Hildegard. This book is intended to contribute to that cause. The reader will find here an overview of Hildegard's life and activity; a dozen meditations, by Matthew Fox, on the texts and illuminations of Hildegard's visions; and a discussion, by Barbara Newman, of Hildegard's music, with lyrics for all the *Vision* tracks, and commentary on each. Fox reflects on Hildegard's meaning and value for believers today, while Newman is more concerned to understand Hildegard within her own historical context. I have adapted Fox's text from his *Illuminations of Hildegard of Bingen* (Santa Fe: Bear & Co., 1985), and Newman's from her *Symphonia: A Critical Edition of the* Symphonia armonie celestium revelationum (*Symphony of the Harmony of Celestial Revelations*) (Ithaca and London: Cornell University Press, 1988). Permission by the publishers to reprint these pages is gratefully acknowledged.

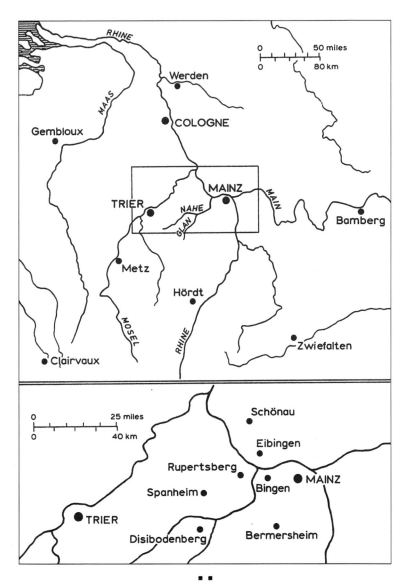

Hildegard's world

VISION

The Life and Music of
Hildegard von Bingen

■ ■

Late-twelfth-century Psalter illumination from southern Germany. A Psalter, or book of Psalms, was Hildegard's early primer, which she used to learn Latin.

CHAPTER ONE

HILDEGARD'S LIFE

Visionary, poet, composer, and healer, Hildegard von Bingen was born in 1098, at Bermersheim bei Alzey, in the diocese of Mainz. Her parents, Hildebert and Mechtilde, were members of the nobility. Little is known about them; the monk Godfrey of Saint Disibod, Hildegard's first biographer, called them "wealthy and engaged in worldly affairs," but that was a standard description in saints' lives, which tended to exaggerate the position of their subjects. Hildegard was Hildebert and Mechtilde's tenth and last child, and thus they offered her to God as a tithe—or at least such was the claim of Guibert of Gembloux, Hildegard's secretary in her last years and the author of another vita, or life, of her.

Hildegard's precarious health and her visionary gift, which was in evidence from earliest childhood, may have influenced her parents' decision to dedicate her to the religious life. At age three, Hildegard told Guibert, she had seen "a brightness so great that [her] soul trembled." This dazzling light, which Hildegard perceived without losing either consciousness or her normal vision (the visionary Elisabeth of Schönau, by contrast, felt her normal senses to be overwhelmed), was combined with clairvoyance. Hildegard was able to tell the color of a calf still in the womb, and to predict the future. As a young girl, however, Hildegard did not yet understand this extraordinary light and the symbolic forms she perceived in it to be gifts from God. Since her visions were accompanied by illness and, as she described it later in life, by "pain so intense that it threaten[ed] to kill [her]," she may even have regarded the visions as a liability. Hildegard's parents perhaps worried that her peculiarities would prevent her from achieving a normal married life, and followed the custom of the time whereby

The Life and Music of Hildegard von Bingen

the nobility sought refuge in monasteries for their weak or handicapped children.

In 1106, the eight-year-old Hildegard was given as a companion to Jutta von Sponheim, a noblewoman who had rejected all offers of marriage and had chosen instead to be enclosed—that is, to be "buried with Christ" and to lead the life of an anchoress, or recluse—in a cell attached to the Benedictine cloister of Saint Disibod. From Jutta, Hildegard learned elementary reading and singing in Latin; her primer was the Psalter, the universal textbook of the Middle Ages. She continued her education with Volmar of Saint Disibod, a monk not much older than Hildegard, who would become her secretary and lifelong friend.

Jutta, as an anchoress, was obliged to remain in her cell until death. Enclosure itself was a kind of death—a death to the world—and the rite by which Jutta had been enclosed employed hymns and responses from the burial service. Her cell, built by her father, was probably located adjacent to the cloister church, so that Jutta could hear the monks singing the *Opus Dei*—the Divine Office, or services of common prayer, prescribed in the Benedictine Rule. But we have no detailed descriptions of the cell. Guibert of Gembloux mentions, in his vita of Hildegard, a small window through which Jutta and her companions could speak to visitors and through which life's necessities were passed (their food likely came from the monastery's kitchens); he describes the women as almost literally enclosed in the cell, with wood and stone solidly wedged together and all entries blocked. The women probably occupied their days with a combination of prayer, meditation, and manual work, such as sewing or copying the Scriptures. Because of their noble birth, Jutta and Hildegard might have had a personal servant with them in the cell.

As other daughters of the local nobility were sent to Saint Disibod, Jutta's hermitage gradually grew into a small convent observing the Benedictine Rule. This development might have brought Hildegard some expertise in musical production, for the increased numbers meant that the women could perform the *Opus*

*The divine marriage, or mystic embrace with Christ, symbolized
by the passion of Kunigunde, Abbess of Saint George and
daughter of King Ottokar II of Bohemia. Fourteenth-
century manuscript illumination.*

Dei themselves rather than depend on the monks. Hildegard made her profession of virginity in her teens (ca. 1113), and received the veil from Otto, bishop of Bamberg. And in 1136, at Jutta's death, Hildegard was the unanimous choice of the sisters to replace Jutta as *magistra*, or abbess, of their community. Though Saint Disibod was now a double monastery (such double monasteries were not uncommon among the Benedictines, especially in Germany), the women's community was subordinate to the men's. Hildegard and her nuns remained dependent on the monks of Saint Disibod not only for the services of a priest but also in all financial and administrative matters.

The real turning point in Hildegard's life came not with her election to abbess but a few years later, in 1141, when she experienced a vision of blinding light, accompanied by a divine call to "tell and write" what she saw and heard in her visions. From childhood, Hildegard had been embarrassed by her strange experiences and, uncertain of their nature, had ceased to mention them to anyone except Jutta, who in turn had confided them to Volmar. Now, too, Hildegard resisted revealing her visions, "on account of humility" and because the call was followed by an illness that she interpreted as a sign of God's displeasure. Finally, however, with the encouragement and assistance of Volmar and the nun Richardis von Stade, Hildegard began her first major visionary work, *Scivias* (*Know the Ways*; Hildegard's title is apparently a contraction of *Scito vias Domini*, "Know the ways of the Lord"). Hildegard wrote down her visions herself, rather than dictate them to a male intermediary, and Volmar served as her copy editor.

Hildegard's most famous work, *Scivias* consists of three sections, each made up of a series of visions—six, seven, and thirteen, respectively. In each case, Hildegard first describes her vision and then presents an exegesis delivered, she says, by a "voice from heaven" (formulas such as "And I heard a voice from heaven saying to me . . ." mark the passage in the text from vision to explication). Her themes are many: the Trinity, the creation, the fall of Lucifer and the subsequent fall of Adam, the Incarnation, evil and

*A scribe. Detail from a French manuscript illumination,
circa 1235. Hildegard wrote the descriptions of her
visions herself, but her longtime friend, secretary,
and former teacher, Volmar of Saint Disibod,
served as her editor.*

The gravestone of Countess Berta of Biburg. Berta, who died in 1151, was a contemporary of Hildegard's. The countess, a very religious woman, founded the cloister of Biburg in Germany.

temptation, the Church and its sacraments, the work of the Holy Spirit, wisdom viewed as human knowledge illumined by faith, the steps by which man will be saved, and the Last Judgment.

No less than other prophets who found fault with their societies, in *Scivias* Hildegard criticizes hers, discoursing at length on the priesthood (many parish priests lacked education, fathered children, and were derelict in their duties), marriage and procreation (toward which Hildegard had a generally positive attitude), and sexuality. It is especially interesting, given the circumstances of Hildegard's entrance into conventual life, that she both condemns the practice of using the monastery as an escape from illness or other worldly troubles and objects to the forcible dedication of children to the religious life.

Scivias ends with a description of a vast "edifice of salvation"—the City of God—and with a version of Hildegard's morality play *Ordo virtutum* (*Play of the Virtues*), which she later set to music and which was intended for performance by her nuns. In the play, the oldest of its kind, the dramatis personae are allegorical virtues, dwelling within the City of God, who help a penitent soul to resist temptation and find salvation. *Scivias* is, in essence, a book of instruction in how best to live life so that one may enter the City of God.

Though it was God who had commanded her to write, six years later, in 1147, Hildegard sought the Church's endorsement of her venture. Still questioning the wisdom of recording her visions, and wondering if remaining silent wasn't the better course after all, Hildegard wrote for guidance to Bernard of Clairvaux, one of the most illustrious preachers and monks of the Middle Ages, and a figure of immense authority. Bernard not only encouraged Hildegard to continue writing but also interceded on her behalf with Pope Eugenius III, who, like Bernard, belonged to the Cistercian monastic order. From Volmar to Abbot Kuno of Saint Disibod, and from Abbot Kuno to Archbishop Heinrich of Mainz, word of Hildegard's visions had reached the pope at a synod of bishops at Trier in 1147–48. Trier was not far from Saint

Pope Eugenius III. Woodcut from
Le vite di tutti i pontefici, *Venice,*
1592. Eugenius III, who was pope
from 1145 to 1153, ratified
Hildegard's visionary gift when
he sent her a letter of approval
to write about her visions.

Disibod, and Eugenius sent a commission to investigate Hildegard's visions and obtain a copy of her writings. Upon receipt of
the still incomplete *Scivias*, Eugenius read from it to the synod.
The members were impressed, and Bernard, who was among the
assembled prelates, used the occasion to suggest that the pope send
Hildegard a letter of approval, authorizing her to continue tran-
scribing her visions. Eugenius did so. Though the papal approval
did not greatly hasten the completion of *Scivias*—Hildegard
would finish it only in 1151—it had an immediate effect on Hildegard's reputation: she became a celebrity.

Hildegard's fame attracted so many postulants to the convent
at Saint Disibod that there was no longer room to house them.
Plans for expanding the nuns' quarters were under way when
Hildegard received a new command from God. This time, she
was directed to move her community to the Rupertsberg, a hill at
the confluence of the Nahe and Rhine rivers, near Bingen. The

*Saint Bernard, Abbot of Clairvaux (1090–1153). Illumination
from Jean Fouquet,* Heures d'Etienne Chevalier. *Bernard
was an abbot and theologian who figured prominently
in the Cistercian movement of church reform.*

A drawing of the Rupertsberg community as it appeared at its apex about 1600. Hildegard built the Rupertsberg in 1152 from the buildings remaining from the time of Saint Rupert. The Rupertsberg, unfortunately, was burned to the ground during war with Sweden in 1632.

Rupertsberg was the site of the tomb of Saint Rupert, who, according to Hildegard's vita of him, had been the grandson of a Carolingian prince, and the son of a pagan father and a Christian mother. (Hildegard not only wrote a life of Rupert but also dedicated the longest and most elaborate of her liturgical songs to him.) When he was fifteen, Rupert made a pilgrimage to Rome; upon his return, he began to give his property away to the poor and to build churches. Rupert had died at twenty, and his mother had erected a monastery at his grave. That monastery was now in ruins—it had been destroyed by the Normans ca. 882—and Hildegard was determined to rebuild it.

The monks of Saint Disibod were against the move to the Rupertsberg. Hildegard's celebrity had brought the monks both reflected spiritual glory and increased material wealth; many of the now numerous visitors left gifts, and the new nuns contributed dowries upon entering the convent. When the nuns and their families also voiced opposition, Hildegard took to her bed, where she lay without speaking or moving. Godfrey's life of Hildegard claims that she finally triumphed when Abbot Kuno, visiting her bedside and finding himself unable to lift Hildegard's head or turn her body, became convinced that her illness was a sign of God's displeasure at the delay in the fulfillment of His will, and at last consented to the move. Hildegard's support was, however, not only divine; she also had the aid of the Countess Richardis von Stade (the mother of the nun who was Hildegard's assistant), who pled Hildegard's case before Archbishop Heinrich of Mainz. The archbishop, in turn, helped Hildegard to purchase the site at the Rupertsberg from its owners, who included the canons of Mainz Cathedral.

In 1150, Hildegard moved to the Rupertsberg with some twenty of her nuns. The early years on the Rupertsberg were difficult ones: the initial poverty of the new convent caused some nuns to leave (even Richardis von Stade was among the defectors), and Hildegard struggled to increase the sisters' independence from the Saint Disibod monks. All the while her health continued to go up and down, depending on the success or failure of her efforts. Only in 1158 did she reach an agreement with Archbishop Arnold of Mainz (Heinrich's successor), wherein he granted Hildegard's convent his protection and agreed to regulate the spiritual relations and the distribution of assets between the Rupertsberg and Saint Disibod communities.

The increased financial and administrative control achieved by Hildegard was accompanied by other, more unusual expressions of autonomy. At the new convent, though they continued to follow the Benedictine Rule, the nuns developed their own distinctive forms of worship and of dress. The latter included "tiaras" or "crowns" directly inspired by one of Hildegard's visions, in which such head coverings were emblems of the blessed virgins in heaven.

With the Rupertsberg on firmer footing, in 1158 Hildegard began her second major work, the *Liber vitae meritorum* (*The Book of Life's Merits*); she completed it in 1163. Like *Scivias*, the *Liber vitae meritorum* consists of a series of visions (in this case, only six) and glosses on them. Here, all of the visions are variations on one theme—that of a man, with his head and shoulders rising into the ether and his feet planted in the watery abyss, who turns from one point of the compass to the next, observing the interrelation of light and darkness. In each of the book's first five sections, a vision of this figure is followed by a dialogue between a group of vices and the corresponding virtues; by explication of Hildegard's vision, mixed with theological commentary; and by a description both of the penalties sinners incur by these vices and of the penances (such as fasting, flagellation, prayer, and—in grave instances—hair shirts and isolation) that expiate them. Hildegard presents the vices in allegorical form, as grotesques whose features mirror their moral deformity. The vice of self-pity (*infelicitas*) is a leper who wears only leaves and beats his breast, while witchcraft (*maleficium*) has a wolf's head, a dog's body, and a lion's tail. In all, thirty-five pairs of vices and virtues are represented—many more than the original seven pairs in the Christian poet Prudentius's

Psychomachia. (Among the most widely read books of the Middle Ages, *Psychomachia* depicted the struggle of Christendom with paganism under the allegory of the struggle between the virtues and the vices. Though Hildegard did not share Prudentius's intent, some of her allegorical personifications do hark back to his work.) In the sixth and final section of the *Liber vitae meritorum*, Hildegard's catalogue of vices yields to more general themes, among them the promise, for the blessed, of the City of God.

During the 1150s, Hildegard's writing zeal found other outlets as well, including two companion volumes dealing with natural science, *Physica (Natural History)* and *Causae et curae (Causes and Cures)*. The first was a scientific and medical encyclopedia, including an herbal, a bestiary, and a lapidary, and the second was a handbook of physical and mental diseases and their remedies, with extensive material on sexuality. These works are remarkable in Hildegard's oeuvre, inasmuch as they are not presented in visionary form and make no claim to divine inspiration. Scholars have been unable to determine which portions of these works represent Hildegard's practical experience, and which portions are derived from the standard medical lore of her time.

In the *Physica*, Hildegard rated the medicinal efficacy of plants according to the four elemental qualities—hot, cold, moist, and dry—traditionally ascribed to created things and linked to the four humors, or temperaments, in man (an imbalance of the humors produced illness). Tormentil, for example, was cold, and Hildegard advocated its use to fight fever: it should be cooked in wine, with some honey, and the concoction drunk at night. Tansy, described as hot and a bit moist, would relieve catarrh. Trees were hot or cold depending on the size and quantity of the fruit they produced; evergreens had particular heat and were able to ward off evil spirits.

■ ■

OPPOSITE: *A depiction of the scriptorium in the tower of the monastery of Tavara. The scriptorium was a room set apart in medieval monasteries where monks would copy manuscripts.*

The Life and Music of Hildegard von Bingen

17

In her catalogue of animals in the *Physica*, Hildegard devoted generous space to fish—which is not surprising, given the significance of fish in the medieval diet, and in the religious diet in particular. She described such birds as the sparrow hawk, which figured in a cure for lustfulness, and the ostrich, which she recommended as a remedy for epilepsy and melancholy. On the subject of insects, she cautioned that flies should not be inadvertently swallowed, but advocated a procedure whereby live glowworms tied in a cloth were pressed to the stomach of an epileptic. Earthworms, Hildegard said, made the best medicine not when dug out of the ground but when they emerged themselves, after a downpour.

Hildegard also prescribed metals and gemstones to treat illness. In the *Physica* she applied the classification of hot and cold to eight metals, and in many of her remedies called for the ingestion of powdered metal. She offered both a scientific and a theological account of the origins of precious stones. The scientific theory was that gems came from the East and represented the crystallized froth of mountain stones that had been heated by the sun to the melting point and then washed by boiling floodwaters. The theological explanation was that precious stones had dropped from Lucifer as he fell from heaven so that their virtue and beauty might be bestowed on Adam and his descendants. Hildegard recommended the external application of the stone or the ingestion of wine in which the gem had been left to soak. The emerald was useful for many ailments—heart pain, headache, and colds, among them—although in some cases the patient needed only to look at an emerald while reciting a religious charm to be cured. A sapphire, if held briefly in the mouth first thing in the morning, would improve one's intellectual powers. Such jewel therapy was, however, probably not much practiced at either the Rupertsberg or other monasteries.

The image of jewels as crystallizations of liquid substances appears in a hymn of Hildegard's, "O ignee Spiritus, laus tibi sit" ("O fiery Spirit, praise be to you"). Christ's wounds had long been symbolically identified with jewels, and the hymn's final image is one of the transformation of men's wounds (that is, sins) into precious stones (the virtues of the soul). Medieval poets also commonly used the gem or crystal as an analogy for the Virgin Birth, an image one encounters in another of Hildegard's songs, the antiphon "O splendidissima gemma" ("O resplendent jewel").

In *Causae et curae*, as in the *Physica*, Hildegard the prophet turned into Hildegard the physician. Here she candidly discussed such subjects as sexual desire, sexual pleasure, intercourse, conception, childbirth, and the differences between the sexes. The society of the Middle Ages was not particularly repressed, and medieval discussions of sex were less euphemistic than any save those of our own times. Hildegard's views on sexual matters are, however, complex and full of anomalies. They are an idiosyncratic and at times self-contradictory combination of conventional theories and her own female visionary intuition, a mix of moral prescriptions and frank, morally neutral naturalism. Though Hildegard took a very optimistic and life-affirming view of sex, she also believed that lovemaking had changed greatly—something had been lost—as a consequence of the Fall. Though she listed mutual desire as a prerequisite for conception, she also insisted that conception could not occur without the cooperation of both God and the devil. She enumerated various circumstances of conception—the strength of the man's semen, the love between man and woman, the phases of the moon—that determined the characteristics of the child. She compared man's desire to a brushfire, woman's to continuous but gentle sunlight. This assertion went against the accepted wisdom of Hildegard's day, which held that women were more lustful than men. Yet one also finds in *Causae et curae* lyrical and even erotic passages about the union of men and women and about the sexual act from the woman's point of view. The knowledge that informs these passages, scholars suppose, came from Hildegard's experience as confidante and counselor to laywomen. *Causae et curae* also includes a catalogue of character types that, unlike the standard personality classifications of the time, emphasized psychosexual traits and offered separate character sketches for men and women. Though she employed the

The Life and Music of Hildegard von Bingen

Ous ceulx qui ce liure veul
lent entendre doiuent sa
uoir que quant maistre pi
erre abaielart eut longue
ment regne et vse de ses arts sa conscien
ce le reprist Il fonda vne abbaye pres

*Abélard and Héloïse confer with an abbess. Many
secular women sought Hildegard's advice on
medical and sexual matters.*

traditional rubrics whereby personalities were judged "sanguine," "phlegmatic," "choleric," or "melancholic," Hildegard's schemas seem based on observation of the real women around her and might have served as a practical guide to help women decide whether to take the veil.

Two of Hildegard's most curious pieces of writing date from the same period: the *Lingua ignota* (*Unknown Language*), a glossary of some nine hundred invented, faintly Germanic-sounding names for both earthly things and celestial beings, and the *Litterae ignotae* (*Unknown Writing*), an alternative alphabet of twenty-three characters. The *Lingua ignota* gives terms for such items as the habits worn by the nuns and the herbs they grew in the Rupertsberg garden. Together, these words represented, perhaps, a secret language for the initiated that, along with the unique practices instituted by Hildegard, contributed to a certain mystical atmosphere in the convent. Five words from the *Lingua ignota* made their way into Hildegard's extremely cryptic votive antiphon "O orzchis Ecclesia" ("O measureless Church"): *orzchis* ("measureless"), *caldemia* ("fragrance"), *loifolum* ("nations"), *crizanta* ("anointed"), and *chorzta* ("sparkling"). That liturgical song is one of the hymns and sequences that make up Hildegard's *Symphonia armonie celestium revelationum* (*Symphony of the Harmony of Celestial Revelations*), on which she was also at work during the 1150s.

Hildegard, who had never studied either singing or musical notation, had begun to compose music in the 1140s. She had not, however, set out to create a song cycle. Only in the late 1150s, by which time she had written a substantial number of lyrics, did she collect and arrange them. These lyrics had been composed in forms, such as responsories and antiphons, that were used in the performance of the *Opus Dei* or of the Mass. Hildegard wrote her music, that is, in response to the needs of the Rupertsberg community. Her subjects included God, the Holy Spirit, the creation, the Virgin Mary and the Incarnation, the coming of Christ, angels, patriarchs, martyrs, Saint Rupert, Saint Ursula, Saint Disibod, Saint Boniface, and John the Baptist.

As an ordered cycle of texts and music, the *Symphonia* survives in two manuscript editions that differ greatly in structure and content. As a result, description of Hildegard's original arrangement of the *Symphonia* remains conjectural. The first version, known as the Dendermonde manuscript, was prepared at the Rupertsberg, under Hildegard's supervision, about 1175; this copy, from which many folios are missing, preserves fifty-seven songs. The second version, the so-called Riesenkodex, consists of more than four hundred leaves of parchment containing Hildegard's collected works, and was prepared with a view to her canonization. It was also produced at the Rupertsberg, but in the 1180s, after Hildegard's death. It contains seventy-five songs, including Hildegard's late compositions. The structure of the *Symphonia*—the order of its sections, and the arrangement of songs within those sections—differs from one manuscript to the other and scholars have disagreed about how to reconcile the two versions and whether to include in the *Symphonia* a scattering of songs from other sources.

Throughout her life, Hildegard engaged in a voluminous correspondence. She exchanged letters with, among others, Bernard of Clairvaux, Popes Anastasius IV and Adrian IV (the successors to Eugenius III), the Holy Roman emperor Frederick Barbarossa, the German king Conrad III, Count Philip of Flanders, and the younger nun and visionary Elisabeth of Schönau, who modeled herself on Hildegard.

In the Middle Ages, it was commonly believed that one could compensate for one's own shortcomings by drawing on the holiness of another; one could be virtuous, that is, by association. Thus regardless of their status—whether they were well born or humble, leaders of the Church or of the state, clergy or laity—Hildegard's correspondents sent her similar solicitations: either general requests for prayers and words of encouragement or consolation, or petitions for specific answers to questions of importance to the writer. Many abbots and abbesses wanted to know, for instance, whether they should persevere in their administrative

*The Holy Roman emperor Frederick I, known as Frederick Barbarossa,
who reigned from 1152 to 1190. From a twelfth-century
manuscript. Frederick was one of Hildegard's
many correspondents.*

duties or step down, so as to have more time for contemplation; one abbess asked to be received into Hildegard's community. Hildegard's guidance was sought in matters of theology, scholastic philosophy, personal salvation, monastic discipline, and the

A seventeenth-century Italian
engraving of Frederick I.

organization of the Church. Once, she was even asked to restore a woman's fertility. Many correspondents requested that Hildegard look into the future and report back to them what she saw.

Between 1158 and 1160, Hildegard undertook the first of four preaching journeys. Her decision to do so was accompanied, as was commonly the case with Hildegard, by a prolonged illness. Having been cloistered for over fifty years, but with her charismatic personality now firmly established, Hildegard took the highly unconventional step of visiting monastic communities in Mainz, Wertheim, Würzburg, Kitzingen, Ebrach, and Bamberg.

In the chapter house of the monastery, or possibly in the monastery church, she gave sermons, often apocalyptic in tone, in which she reprimanded lax clergy and advocated monastic and clerical reform.

Saint Rupert of Salzburg, from the World Chronicle *by Schedel, 1495. Hildegard was a great admirer of Saint Rupert, writing a vita of him, founding the Rupertsberg in his honor, and composing a liturgical song for him. Saint Rupert was an eighth-century missionary bishop who evangelized the Germans.*

Monastic life in Hildegard's time, it should be noted, did not necessarily entail a life of poverty. Wealthy families gave monasteries land and goods in exchange for spiritual favors. The heads of religious houses could also be powerful figures in their own right, with sizable incomes from their estates. In general, life in the monasteries mirrored the social conventions of the wider secular world—even in Hildegard's Rupertsberg convent. The nuns of aristocratic background kept apart from those who were low born, and it was these who performed most of the manual labor.

On her second tour, in 1160, Hildegard stopped in Metz and

Krauftal; in Trier she preached in public (few women were accorded such a privilege), and again she called on the leaders of the Church to reform themselves. In 1163, on her third tour, Hildegard is said to have visited Cologne, Boppard, Andernach, Siegburg, Werden, and Liège. On her last journey, to Swabia in 1170, she traveled to a series of monasteries, including Maulbronn, Hirsau, Kirchheim, Zwiefalten, and Hördt.

In 1163, Hildegard began *De operatione Dei* (*On the Activity of God*), known also as the *Liber divinorum operum* (*The Book of Divine Works*)—the third and final volume in her visionary trilogy. Her work on the book was often interrupted, and it was not completed until about 1174. Hildegard often put *De operatione Dei* aside in favor of shorter projects, which included expositions of the Benedictine Rule and the Athanasian Creed, and lives of Saint Rupert and Saint Disibod.

Renewal of the cult of Saint Rupert had been an aim of Hildegard's ever since she moved her convent to the Rupertsberg, and her vita of Rupert may have been designed to enhance his reputation at a time when Hildegard was seeking to transfer property from the Saint Disibod to the Rupertsberg monastery—an effort in which she was successful.

It was Abbot Helenger (Kuno's successor) of the Saint Disibod cloister who commissioned the vita of Disibod, a seventh-century saint. In her account, Hildegard described the bishop Disibod's exile from his see in Ireland and his journey to Germany, his founding of the monastery and his life of solitude in a hermitage he built on the mountainside, his death at the age of eighty-one, and the miraculous healings that occurred at his tomb. Hildegard also celebrated Saint Disibod in several of the hymns in her *Symphonia*.

De operatione Dei is made up of ten visions, divided into three sections of unequal length. The first five visions (sections one and two) chart the relation of man and nature. Hildegard describes the influence of the winds and the planets on the welfare of human beings, and the relation between the seasons of the year and the ages

■ ■

The Wheel of Life, *Hildegard's vision
of the interconnection of microcosm
and macrocosm.*

of man. She draws an analogy between the seas and rivers of the
earth and the veins of the human body. And she discusses both the
structure of the earth and the spiritual significance of the arrangement of the organs in the body.

The last five visions, in the third section, turn to history—the
history of the world and the history of salvation (the contest, that
is, between God and the devil)—and culminate in the Last Judgment. The text of *De operatione Dei* also includes two long com-
mentaries, one on the prologue of Saint John's Gospel (John
1:1–14) and the other on the first chapter of Genesis. Throughout *De operatione Dei*, Hildegard's theme is that of the relationship
of man and universe as microcosm and macrocosm: in one of her
visions, Hildegard represents the universe as a wheel located in the
breast of the figure of Caritas, or Divine Love; at the center of the
wheel stands a human being, preeminent among created things.

The Life and Music of Hildegard von Bingen

The Abbey of Saint Hildegard in Eibingen, Germany. It is one of the abbeys Hildegard founded; the abbey is still in operation today.

R exrogat Abbatem. Mathildim Supplicat atr;

The Holy Roman emperor Henry IV asking the Abbot of Cluny and
Matilda of Tuscany to intercede for him with Pope Gregory VII, who
had excommunicated Henry in 1076. Henry reigned until 1106,
the year Hildegard was given over to monastic life by her parents.
His reign and that of his son were marked by civil and religious strife.
However, the turn of the twelfth century also witnessed church
reform and the founding of new religious orders.

In 1165, the prosperity of the Rupertsberg community was such that Hildegard was able to found a second convent, at Eibingen, across the Rhine from Bingen. The daughter house at Eibingen still operates, as the Abbey of Saint Hildegard, but the original Rupertsberg convent was destroyed during the Thirty Years War. Twice a week, Hildegard traveled by boat across the Rhine between the two houses. During these boat rides, she was said to have cured the blind by the application of river water. Hildegard, in fact, enjoyed a wide reputation as a healer. This was a traditional role for women, and especially for nuns, who grew therapeutic plants in their cloister gardens. About 1169, Hildegard even acted as an exorcist—a role that was reserved for men in the Church—in the case of a young noblewoman from Cologne who had been possessed by the devil for eight years. According to the letters to and from Hildegard that record this incident, the exorcism was a success, and the young woman, once she was freed from Satan's hold, became a member of Hildegard's community.

Two crises shaped the last years of Hildegard's life. In 1173, Volmar died. Volmar had been secretary to Hildegard and both provost and spiritual father to the Rupertsberg convent. The abbot of Saint Disibod, whose duty it was to provide a replacement, did not hurry to do so. Aside from Hildegard's personal loss, the loss of their provost was a problem for the cloister members. Hildegard turned to Pope Alexander III for help and, after protracted negotiations, a new provost, Godfrey, was sent from Saint Disibod. Godfrey began to write his vita of Hildegard while at the Rupertsberg, but he died without finishing it, in 1176. In 1177, Godfrey's place was taken by Guibert of Gembloux, who remained at the convent until after Hildegard's death.

Hildegard had her last, and most serious, wrangle with her ecclesiastical superiors in 1178, when her convent was placed under interdict. A grave sanction, the interdict meant that Mass could not be celebrated at the convent, the nuns could not receive the sacraments, and the *Opus Dei* could be whispered behind closed doors but not chanted—there could, that is, be no music. The offense that prompted this grave punishment was that the Ruperts-berg nuns buried in their churchyard a nobleman who the clergy of Mainz claimed had died excommunicate. Mainz demanded that the body be disinterred. Hildegard refused, saying that before his death the man had been reconciled to the Church and that exhumation of his body would be a terrible sin. This confrontation produced an extraordinary document, a letter from Hildegard to the Mainz prelates, in which, opposing the interdict, she argued that music and song have a high place in divine worship and in the divine plan, and that those who silence the Church in its praise of God do so at their own peril. "So you and all prelates," Hildegard wrote, "must use the greatest vigilance before stopping, by decree, the mouth of any assembly of people singing to God . . . you must always beware lest in your judgment you are ensnared by Satan, who drew man out of the celestial harmony and the delights of paradise." The interdict was finally lifted in March 1179. Six months later, on September 17, 1179, Hildegard died.

In 1233, Pope Gregory IX began proceedings for Hildegard's canonization. The effort foundered, however, since investigators were careless in their recording of the dates and places of miracles attributed to Hildegard, and of the names of witnesses to them. Among the witnesses were three of Hildegard's nuns, who asserted that they had seen Hildegard illumined by the Holy Spirit as she walked through the Rupertsberg cloister, chanting one of her musical compositions. Nonetheless, in the fourteenth century Hildegard's name began to appear in martyrologies and in 1324 Pope John XXII gave permission for her "solemn and public cult." Hildegard's feast is celebrated in the Catholic dioceses of Germany on September 17, the anniversary of her death.

■ ■

OPPOSITE: *Modern-day mural of Saint Hildegard, on Basilika Street in Bingen, Germany.*

SANCTA·HILDEGARDIS
ANNO 1098-1179

CHAPTER TWO

HILDEGARD'S VISIONS

By far the best account of Hildegard's visions comes in a letter Hildegard wrote in 1175, when she was seventy-seven, to the monk Guibert of Gembloux:

> In [my visions] my soul . . . rises up high into the vault of heaven and into the changing sky and spreads itself out among different peoples, although they are very far away from me in distant lands and places. And because I see them this way in my soul, I observe them in accord with the shifting of clouds and other created things. I do not hear them with my outward ears, nor do I perceive them by the thoughts of my own heart or by any combination of my five senses, but in my soul alone, while my outward eyes are open. So I have never fallen prey to ecstasy in the visions, but I see them wide awake, day and night. . . .
>
> The light that I see thus is not spatial, but it is far, far brighter than a cloud that carries the sun. I can measure neither height, nor length, nor breadth in it; and I call it "the reflection of the living Light." And as the sun, the moon, and the stars appear in water, so writings, sermons, virtues, and certain human actions take form for me and gleam within it.

As for the translation of her visions into words, Hildegard explained in the same letter,

> . . . what I write is what I see and hear in the vision. I compose no other words than those I hear, and I set them forth in unpolished Latin just as I hear them in the vision, for I am not taught in this vision to write as philosophers do. And the

words in the vision are not like words uttered by the mouth of man, but like a shimmering flame, or a cloud floating in a clear sky.

Hildegard offered no comment, however, on the rendering of her words back into images—via the illumination of her writings.

About 1165, an illuminated manuscript of *Scivias* was prepared at Hildegard's scriptorium at the Rupertsberg convent. It is likely that Hildegard supervised the work of the unidentified artist, who was possibly one of her nuns. The illuminations are unusual and often startling; they are reminiscent of woodcuts and do not share the style of contemporary manuscript painting. Traditionally distinct scenes are sometimes compressed in them—the miniature *The Fall*, for instance, combines in a single image the creation of Eve and the temptation—and the effect of this condensation can be to make the illuminations' symbolism obscure. Moreover, the artist sometimes departs from Hildegard's text. This is the case in *The Mystical Body*, where Hildegard's vision of Ecclesia, the virgin Church, as a queen clothed in many colors (with each color representing an order within the Church), has yielded an image of Ecclesia lifting her arms to heaven, her breast aflame with love and her heart crowded with monks and virgins. Color, finally, is not without its meaning in the illuminations: though red, blue, and gold predominate, the rare *viriditas*, or fresh green, represents the life, growth, and fertility that flow from the power of God.

The whereabouts of the original illuminated manuscript of *Scivias* are unknown: the manuscript was taken to Dresden for safekeeping during the Second World War, and has been missing ever since. During the late 1920s, however, the nuns at Eibingen had prepared a complete facsimile, and it is from this copy, housed now in the Hessische Landesbibliothek in Wiesbaden, that the *Scivias* illuminations are reproduced here.

An illuminated manuscript of *De operatione Dei* was prepared in the thirteenth century, after Hildegard's death. This manuscript, which was probably not produced at the Rupertsberg, is now in the collection of the Bibliotèca Statale di Lucca, in Italy. Here, too, the artist, who succeeds brilliantly at capturing the details of Hildegard's visions, is anonymous.

The commentary below, on nine illuminations from *Scivias* and three from *De operatione Dei*, is by Matthew Fox.* All quotations are from Hildegard's writings. The brief titles given to the images follow those adopted in the German-language editions of Hildegard's texts.

---

*Adapted from Matthew Fox, *Illuminations of Hildegard of Bingen* (Santa Fe: Bear & Co., 1985).

The Life and Music of Hildegard von Bingen

The Seer
De operatione Dei

In this picture Hildegard celebrates her conversion experience. It was art—that is, self-expression—that was the ultimate form of healing for Hildegard. She describes her condition of passivity, being without voice, frustrated, physically sick. In the name of humility she had made herself sick. "Not in stubbornness but in humility, I refused to write for so long that I felt pressed down under the whip of God into a bed of sickness." She tells us that even though she had experienced wonderful things, "because of doubt and erroneous thinking and because of controversial advice from men," she had refused to write. "Beaten down by many kinds of illnesses, I put my hand to writing. Once I did this . . . I received the strength to rise up from my sickbed, and under that power I continued to carry out the work to the end, using all of ten years to do it." By putting her hand to writing, by self-expression, by art as meditation, Hildegard finally achieved strength and power.

Hildegard does not hesitate to appropriate the Pentecost experience, the Holy Spirit's fire that illumines and thaws and connects. It was when she was "inflamed by a fiery light" that she began writing. The parted tongues of fire are clearly a reference to the first Christian disciples' experience of Pentecost. The first disciples, like Hildegard, were cured of their doubt and fear so as to preach the Good News (Acts 2:9–11). In picturing herself as a recipient of the Pentecostal fire, Hildegard refers to her own missionary activity and prophetic vocation.

The monk depicted in the picture is Hildegard's secretary, Volmar.

Steadfastness During Temptation
Scivias

We are subjected to many trials in this life—"as long as a person lives in soul and body, many invisible trials disturb the soul of that person." We are called to "hurl away the deceits of the devil." But many times "God hurls tempests on humans" and we who are "fragile in flesh" cry out: "I have such great and heavy things weighing my flesh down. I am not strong enough to overcome myself." What is needed on our part? Strength. It is the strength of the woman and soul depicted in this vision that Hildegard calls us to. "When you oppose the devil the way a strong warrior opposes his enemy, then God is delighted with your struggle and wishes you to call upon him constantly in all hours in your distress." In the picture there are many "storms" and enemies that are hostile to the woman, who wish "to hurl her down. But they are not strong enough." That soul "resists strongly" and guards itself with heavenly inspiration. We are to be like her, grounded in strength. "Become strong, therefore, and be comforted, because this is necessary for you."

How often Hildegard speaks of the strength of Saint Ursula and her friends, martyred for their faith. Hildegard wrote poems and songs about Ursula, celebrating her strong soul, her cosmic beauty. "The devil possessed their bodies and they slaughtered those maidens in all their noble grace." We who have lived through the martyrdom of so many in our century understand the deep meaning of what Hildegard symbolizes in the murder of Ursula and her companions.

Man and Universe
De operatione Dei

Hildegard sees "a wheel of marvelous appearance . . . right in the center of the breast" of a towering figure. Who is the figure holding the wheel? It is "a wondrously beautiful image within the mystery of God. It had a human form, and its countenance was of such beauty and radiance that I could have more easily gazed at the sun than at that face." Who is the figure? "Love appearing in a human form, the Love of our heavenly Father . . . Love—in the power of the everlasting Godhead."

The entire cosmos now rests within the bosom of the Creator. The cosmos is surrounded by "luminous fire" on the outside and by "black fire" on the inside, and by a watery air that "moistens all the other circles with dampness."

In the center of the giant wheel there is a human figure, and in what Hildegard calls the "cosmic wheel" are the heads of animals breathing onto the human figure: leopard, wolf, lion, bear, stag, crab, serpent, and lamb. Seven planets exist in the various circles and "all the planets shone their rays at the animal heads as well as at the human figure." Sixteen major stars appear within the circle and other, lesser, stars fill the circles of air.

How does Hildegard interpret the human figure in this vision? She is now expounding on the relation of microcosm and macrocosm. The human body, for Hildegard, is in the cosmos, and the cosmos is in the human body. One forms the other. Hildegard says: "Humanity stands in the midst of the structure of the world. . . . Its head is turned upward and its feet toward the solid ground, and it can place into motion both the higher and the lower things. Whatever it does . . . permeates the universe."

The Wheel of Life
De operatione Dei

In this beautiful mandala and her commentary on it, Hildegard celebrates the deep psychological healing that occurs when microcosm and macrocosm are wedded again. We see in this cosmic wheel humans cultivating the earth through the seasons of the year and the seasons of their lives. Hildegard compares the cyclic turn of the seasons to a potter's wheel. "The sun's heat and the moisture of the waters cultivate the whole earth, make it fruitful, and complete it, just as a potter completes his vessels by turning his wheel." And she celebrates the fertility of the earth. "I saw how moisture from the gentle layer of air flowed over the earth. This air revived the earth's greening power and caused all fruits to put forth seeds and become fertile."

Hildegard was truly celebrating life with this vision, for she says "God is life." She knows this from observing the divine brilliance in creatures. "All living creatures are, so to speak, sparks from the radiation of God's brilliance, and these sparks emerge from God like the rays of the sun." She asks a necessary question: "How would God be known as life if not through the fact that the realm of the living, which glorifies and praises God, also emerges from God? On this account God has established the living, burning sparks as a sign of the brilliance of the divine renown."

Hildegard completes her meditation with a lengthy exegesis of the first chapter of Saint John's Gospel. There we are reminded that the light of God (Hildegard might prefer "spark" or "fire" or "flame of God") came into the world to set its tent among us (John 1:14).

The True Trinity in True Unity
Scivias

Hildegard describes this illumination in the following manner: "A most quiet light and in it burning with flashing fire the form of a man in sapphire blue." We experience in this mandala much that is peacemaking and powerful. Hildegard understands this mandala to represent the Divine Trinity. "One light, three persons, one God," she declares.

In another place Hildegard pictures the Trinity in this way: "The Father is brightness and this brightness has a flashing forth and in this flashing forth is fire and these three are one." In this vision, she calls the Creator a "living" light; the Son, "flash of light"; the Spirit, "fire." She says that this fire of the Holy Spirit binds all things together—"The Holy Spirit streams through and ties together 'eternity' and 'equality' so that they are one."

Hildegard's theology of the Trinity, so energetically set forth in this mandala, is about the entrance of divine compassion into the world. Her Christology presented in this picture of the "blue Christ" is rich and clear. Jesus Christ is the revelation of the compassion of God, the incarnation of divine compassion, the human person in whom divine compassion shines forth in a special way. All the Trinitarian energies in this picture find their culmination in the healing and extended hands of the man in sapphire blue.

The gold and silver circles in this image resemble rope. Hildegard herself refers to the "web of the universe" on more than one occasion. Thus her golden rope tells us of the interconnectivity of all being and of divinity with creation and humanity.

Extinguished Stars
Scivias

In this vision Hildegard concentrates on Lucifer's fall. At the top of the picture are the golden stars, the splendid "brightness that spreads itself out everywhere in its fullness, up into the heights of heaven and down into the depths of the abyss." But one star, the brightest of all, whom we call Lucifer ("light bearer"), leaves the multitude, taking other angels with him. "Lucifer the angel, who now is Satan, embellished in his beginning with great glory and clothed with much brightness and beauty, departed from the command of the omnipotent Father. And with him there went all the sparks of his group, shining in the brightness of life at that time. But now, they were extinguished in the darkness of the fog . . . and turned into the blackness of burnt wood."

But brightness, not darkness, dominates this picture. Why? Hildegard teaches that the brightness once belonging to Lucifer has now been taken back by the Creator, who "preserved it in his mystery. For the glory of that brightness ought not to be in vain, so God preserved it for a higher light that was to be made." Who is that? Humanity. Humans are the heirs to the brightness and glory of Lucifer. "I the heavenly God preserved the bright light which withdrew from the devil because of his evil. I concealed this carefully within myself and I gave it to the mud of the earth whom I formed in my image and likeness." All fathers do this when a son dies: they keep that son's inheritance until another is born.

The Fall
Scivias

Here, Hildegard begins with the beauty of creation: the four elements—earth, air, fire, and water—are pictured in the four corners. The stars are alive and shining and fiery and represent the angels: "Thereupon I saw the greatest conceivable multitude of objects like living torches, having a great brightness." These stars "shine in a blessed life and appear in great grace and embellishment" because they "stood firmly in divine love." But one angel, Lucifer, rebelled and sinned.

What happened to Lucifer after the fall? He tumbled into a black lake "great in breadth and depth, having a mouth like the mouth of a well and emitting burning smoke with a great stench." In the lake was the "densest darkness" and, as we can see in Hildegard's picture, the devil takes on the form of a serpent and the dark lake begins to resemble a certain tree.

We also see a garden of delights, and in the midst of this garden is a pair of lovers, Adam and Eve. Hildegard pictures Eve in this vision as a cloud filled with stars, issuing from Adam's rib.

Hildegard subscribes to the thesis that Adam's fall made for even more beauty in the human race and in the coming of Christ. "Humanity shines more splendidly now than it did when it was first created in heaven. . . . This might not have happened if the Son of God had not put on human flesh." Virtues abound now more than previously. Humanity, Hildegard tells us, has been "elevated above the heavens, because God appeared in humanity and humanity in God through the Son of God." God's Son cleansed humanity and placed it "back in its previous honor with even greater glory."

The Redeemer
Scivias

At the top of the picture is a mandala very similar in color and form to Hildegard's image *The True Trinity in True Unity*. Hildegard calls this mandala of fiery, cosmic ropes the "living fire" of the Creator God. The circle also appears to be an eye, and Hildegard refers in this vision to the creation's happening in a blink of the Creator's eye.

In the middle circle Hildegard presents six smaller circles, representing the six days of creation. Read these from left to right beginning at the top. The fingerlike shape protruding into the six days of creation she describes as a whitening and "blazing lightening" which "stirs every creature up." It has an obvious phallic form, but elsewhere too Hildegard talks about "the finger of God which is the Holy Spirit." If you look carefully just below the finger, you will see a lump of red clay with a human head emerging. This is the finger of God breathing life into the first human.

Adam is pictured as being about to slip down into the darkness. But stars appear in the darkness and these, Hildegard instructs, represent Abraham, Isaac, and Jacob, who are "great luminaries." The major and minor prophets are represented by the other stars. John the Baptist is pictured as the living flame beckoning the Christ figure to arrive on the scene. Christ is pictured emerging from Mary's womb, the blue circle at the bottom of the illumination.

The Mystical Body
Scivias

Elsewhere, Hildegard presents this formidable figure of a woman with a fishing net around her. In that vision, Hildegard describes baptism into the Mother Church.

Hildegard describes this vision in the following manner:

> I saw a certain brightness white as snow and like transparent crystal lighting up the . . . image of a woman. She was shining with a reddish gleam like the dawn from her throat to her breasts. . . . And I heard a voice from heaven saying: "This is the flowering on the celestial Zion, the mother and flower of roses and of lilies of the valley. O flowering, you will be betrothed to the son of the most powerful king. You will bear him the most celebrated offspring when you will be comforted in time."

In the forefront of persons in the bosom of the Church is a maiden in red, and surrounding her is "a very great tumult of persons brighter than the sun, all decorated wonderfully with gold and jewels." There is joy and celebration, for "these are the daughters of Zion and with them are the lyres and the musicians who play them and every type of music and the voice of perfect merriment and the joy of joys." They are the virgin martyrs who "courageously overcame death and are most wondrously filled with the highest wisdom."

Christ's Sacrifice and the Church
Scivias

It is noteworthy that among the pictures Hildegard has left us in her books, there is not an isolated one of the Crucifixion of Christ. Only four picture the Crucifixion at all. By far the most prominent exposition of the Cross is in the present vision. Much of Hildegard's meditation on this vision constitutes a commentary on the Mass, which Hildegard sees as a cosmic event that "cheers the inner strength" of persons and sustains them.

In this illumination, we see two pictures. The one on top includes the crucified Christ with the Mother Church whom we have seen in *The Mystical Body*. Hildegard is celebrating the "happy bethrothal" of Christ and Church. "I heard a voice from heaven saying: 'Son, let this woman be a bride to you in the restoration of my people, regenerating souls through the salvation of spirit and water.'" The blood that flows from Christ's side fills the woman's cup. This is her dowry, Hildegard tells us frequently in this passage. The "only begotten of God devoted his body and blood with most distinguished glory to his faithful, who are both the Church and the sons and daughters of the Church so that they may have life in the celestial city through him."

But the vast portion of Hildegard's meditation is not on the upper figure but the lower one. In that figure the cosmic event of the Crucifixion of Christ is played out in human history by way of memory—there are four "mirrors" reminding us of the mysteries of Christ's life—and of worship. Hildegard identifies the four circles or "mirrors" in this vision as images of the nativity, the passion and burial, the resurrection, and the ascension of Christ. And she compares the coming of God's Son at some length to the coming of divinity in the Eucharist. The essence of the Eucharist is to eat and to drink. For this worship is a "true and health-filled meal" and a dinner and a remembrance feast.

The End of Time
Scivias

This vision borrows heavily from the message, the form, the emotion of the Book of the Apocalypse, or the Book of Revelation.

In the upper left-hand corner of this vision we see five animals. Hildegard reports: "Thereupon I looked to the north. And behold five beasts were standing there—a fiery dog that was not burning; a lion that was reddish brown; a pale horse; a black pig; and a grisly wolf." Each had a piece of rope in his mouth. She tells us that the fiery dog stands for humans who "bite at their own condition" and who do not burn with the justice of God. The reddish lion stands for "warlike men" who wage wars without considering God's judgment. The pale horse stands for those who put their own selfish pleasure before the performance of worthwhile acts. The black pig stands for rulers who create sadness and uncleanness in themselves and their subjects. The wolf stands for those who rob others. The black rope, she tells us, represents "the darkness that stretches out many injustices."

In the upper right-hand corner, in the East, sits a "youth clothed in a purple tunic. I had seen this youth before [at] the junction between a bright stone wall and a building." This youth holds a lyre in one hand and has two fingers of the other hand raised. Hildegard celebrates this Christ figure as "the bridegroom of the Church," who is shining splendidly because he "reveals the shining of justice in the righteousness of those who worship him devotedly."

In the bottom left-hand corner we see the familiar form of the woman who is Mother Church. In place of her lower body, a horrible picture emerges. "A monstrous and very black head appeared, having fiery eyes and ears like the ears of an ass and nostrils and mouth like the nostrils and mouth of a lion, crunching with a great jaw." In the right of the picture, an ugly head breaks loose from the Mother figure and, moving with "monstrous ugliness, it spreads a foul stench on the mountain" and "tears the institution of the Church to pieces." This figure is the Antichrist.

But Hildegard does not leave us in a state of despair and defeat. Two witnesses are to rise up, Enoch and Elijah, who will lead the people back from Satan. They are symbolized, Hildegard instructs us, by the two raised fingers of the man on the wall. Hildegard comments that these prophets will "carry the banner of the justice of God" and stabilize believers in their faith and put the devil to flight.

The Life and Music of Hildegard von Bingen

59

The Zeal of God
Scivias

In this vision, Hildegard sees two walls coming together, with a fiery red head at the corner where the walls join. She tells us that the walls, which are two of the four walls of the celestial building or the celestial city, are there for our strength and defense. One wall is smooth and solid and very bright; the other is made up of stones. Hildegard says that the first wall "shines in the brightness of the light of day" and is called "speculative knowledge . . . because through it a person sees and judges his own actions." The second wall symbolizes our works.

Where the two walls meet, there is a "zealous red head." Hildegard describes this head as having "a fiery color, shining red like a flame of fire. It had a terrifying face." It had three wings "of amazing breadth and length which were white as a shining cloud" and these wings grew larger as they beat and beat. The head itself did not speak and did not move. Christ, however, spoke. "This head signifies the zeal of the Lord," Hildegard says.

The zeal of God is essentially justice-making; it comes about when we are aroused by injustice. "In mirror [that is, speculative] knowledge and in human work there is a common boundary of injustice," Hildegard tells us. God cares so much for justice that in the past, under the Old Law of Abraham and Moses as well as in the present, under the New Law of Christ, the divine zeal was always and continues to be for justice.

CHAPTER THREE

HILDEGARD'S MUSIC

BY BARBARA NEWMAN[*]

The *Symphonia* in the Monastic Liturgy

There is no doubt that Hildegard intended her music for Mass and the Divine Office at her monastery. Monastic worship is ordered around the Divine Office, which consists of seven daily "hours," or services of common prayer, plus the night service of matins. The basic structure of these services is set forth in chapters eight through eighteen of the Benedictine Rule. Each hour consists in varying proportions of psalmody, lessons from Scripture, and assorted texts of prayer and praise set to music—canticles, antiphons, responsories, and hymns. The three Gospel canticles are fixed texts, but the other items vary with each

‥

OPPOSITE: *The nave of a Benedictine cloister built circa 1110. All of Hildegard's music was written to be performed in a setting such as this. The mural in the apse of this church, located in Petersberg-bei-Dachau, Germany, shows Christ, the martyrdom of Peter and Paul, and Mary with angels.*

---

[*]This chapter—text, Latin lyrics, and English translations—is adapted from Saint Hildegard of Bingen, *Symphonia: A Critical Edition of the* Symphonia armonie celestium revelationum (*Symphony of the Harmony of Celestial Revelations*), introduction, translations, and commentary by Barbara Newman (Ithaca and London: Cornell University Press, 1988). The commentary on "Cum eruberint" includes material from Marianne Richert Pfau's "Music and Text in Hildegard's Antiphons," included in Newman's edition of the *Symphonia*. Only the prose translations are reproduced here. The Latin text of "O vivens fons" and the commentary on it are from Peter Dronke, *Poetic Individuality in the Middle Ages: New Departures in Poetry, 1000–1150* (Oxford: Clarendon Press, 1970); the English translation is by Peter Dronke, from the record liner for *Hildegard von Bingen: Ordo Virtutum* (Harmonia Mundi 20395/96).

The Life and Music of Hildegard von Bingen

Christ in a mandorla, in
the cloister at Petersberg-bei-
Dachau. Detail of the apse mural.

day and hour and constitute a vast corpus of medieval chant. The
genre most fully represented in the *Symphonia*, as in the chant
repertoire generally, is the *antiphon*. Forty-three of Hildegard's
compositions, well over half, belong to this category, which is related to the practice of psalmody.

In standard medieval usage an antiphon, or freely composed
text with melody, would be sung before and after each psalm in the
Office. Because the Office was designed by Saint Benedict to cover the full cycle of 150 psalms every week, this style of psalmody
required an enormous number of antiphons. Matins in the monastic usage includes as many as twelve psalms, each with its antiphon.
Vespers has up to five, as does the early morning office of lauds;
and each of the lesser hours has three. As the antiphon is liturgi-
cally subordinate to the psalm, it is usually a brief, unpretentious
composition suited to the Scriptural theme or the feast of the day.
It takes its name from the practice of antiphonal singing: psalm
verses would be chanted alternately by two half choirs, while the
antiphon was sung by the full choir to a simple tune related to the

reciting tone. (In more elaborate performance, it might be sung between verses as well as before and after the psalm.)

Not all antiphons were tied to psalmody, however. It became customary to insert somewhat longer, more elaborate antiphons after the Gospel canticles that concluded the major hours, especially the Magnificat at vespers and the Benedictus at lauds. The Marian devotion of the Middle Ages expressed itself richly in these longer "free," or votive, antiphons. Of Hildegard's forty-three antiphons, fourteen appear to be votive antiphons, for in the manuscripts they lack the *differentia*, or cadence, that would connect them with a psalm tone.

The second most frequent item in the *Symphonia* is the *responsory*, represented by eighteen pieces and intended primarily for matins. This service, in the most solemn monastic usage, consists of three sections called nocturns, each nocturn including a group of psalms or canticles, with their antiphons followed by four lessons from Scripture. After each lesson a responsory is sung — a freely composed, musically complex piece that alternates solo verses with choral response. Unlike antiphons, responsories tend to give several notes and sometimes highly embellished melodic phrases to each syllable so that the trained soloists and choirs can display their skill. The textual form is also complex and allows for many structural variants.

In addition to antiphons and responsories, the *Symphonia* includes fourteen longer pieces that are artistically among Hildegard's most accomplished. *Hymns*, which grew out of early Christian congregational singing, were sung at various points in the Office but never at Mass. A typical twelfth-century hymn was a song in which each stanza followed the same metrical pattern and rhyme scheme, and was sung to the same relatively simple tune. *Sequences* developed in the Carolingian period and underwent a complex musical and poetic evolution. Composed by the thousands, they were to be sung between the Alleluia and the Gospel at Mass. Classical sequences are composed of paired versicles rather than stanzas. Following the principle of *strophic responsion*, the two versicles in each pair have the same number of syllables and are sung to the same tune, but the melody and the textual form change from pair to pair. By the twelfth century, however, most new sequences were being composed in stanzaic form and followed a set meter and rhyme scheme, even though their music retained the older strophic responsion.

Hildegard, a maverick, preferred the archaic nonmetrical sequence, but exceeded the Carolingian composers in irregularity. In fact, her forms are so free that it is often hard to tell a sequence from a hymn.

Finally, the *Symphonia* includes two short pieces for Mass: a setting of the Kyrie and the Alleluia verse "O virga mediatrix" ("O branch, mediatrix"), to be sung in place of a sequence before the Gospel.

Musical Style and Performance

Hildegard's creations, compared with a contemporary hymn by Peter Abélard or a sequence by Adam of Saint Victor, will sound either primitive or unnervingly avant-garde. In a sense they are both. As a Benedictine, she was acquainted with a large repertoire of chant, but she lacked formal training and made no attempt to imitate the mainstream poetic and musical achievements of her day. Various scholars have hypothesized that she was influenced by German folk song, yet her compositions lack the two essential traits of a popular tune: it must be easy to remember and easy to sing. The difficult music of the *Symphonia* is sui generis.

One useful way of discussing the style of plainsong is to locate items on a spectrum ranging from simple *syllabic* pieces, in which each syllable is sung to a single note, to ornate *melismatic* chant, in which one syllable may be embroidered with a figure of several notes or even several phrases. In general, the more melismatic a piece, the more solemn, elaborate, and difficult it is, and the more

"De spiritus sanctus," *written by Hildegard. This is an example of the style of musical notation of Hildegard's day.*

the text is dominated by the music. Hildegard's sequences and hymns fall into the intermediate range sometimes called *neumatic*, in which there are seldom more than two or three notes to a syllable. Her antiphons and responsories, however, can be melismatic in the extreme, with the longest melismas falling at the beginning and end of songs as a kind of musical punctuation. The style can be florid, almost rococo, and demands a skillful and well-trained choir.

Another eccentric feature of Hildegard's style is the wide vocal range she employs. Many songs have an ambitus of two octaves and some even of two and a half, placing a considerable strain on the voice of the average singer. Also notable are the wide melodic leaps, especially the frequently ascending and descending fifths. Hildegard had a way of scurrying rapidly up and down the octave, like an angel on Jacob's ladder, several times in the space of a word.

The eight church modes or scales, as Hildegard uses them, tend to collapse into three different tonalities, on D, E, and C. One tonality resembles our major and another our minor scale, the third being the medieval Phrygian mode. In each mode, however, Hildegard drew on a relatively small number of motifs, which she repeated, with ingenious variation, in every piece composed in that mode. This quality of repetition restores some of the musical stability she sacrificed in abandoning strophic construction. But even in her more or less regular hymns and sequences, the repeated melodies are never exactly the same because the text itself is not regular. So to accommodate the uneven numbers of syllables, small melodic motifs are continually interpolated and omitted. As a result, nothing is ever musically predictable. This extreme liberty of construction is the counterweight to Hildegard's motivic style of composition.

There is no answer to the usual vexed question whether the *Symphonia* was performed "rhythmically." As few chant notations supply note values, singers must use their discretion. Nor is there evidence that the songs were accompanied with instruments.

Despite our maddening ignorance about medieval performance practice, it is nonetheless tempting to imagine how the *Symphonia* sounded in situ at the Rupertsberg. Given her visionary conception of music, it is hard to believe that the rhapsodic quality of her lyrics did not call forth a similarly rapt, uninhibited performance style.

Poetic Style

Hildegard's poetic world is like the Sibyl's cave: difficult of access, reverberating with cryptic echoes. The oracle's message, once interpreted, may or may not hold surprises. But the suppliant emerges with a sense of initiation, and the voice itself is unforgettable.

No formal poetry written in the twelfth century, and none that Hildegard might have known, is very much like hers. For models one must look, rather, to the rich corpus of liturgical prayer. It is not surprising that, until the advent of modern vers libre, scholars were reluctant even to dignify Hildegard's songs with the title of poetry. In style they are much closer to *Kunstprosa*, a highly wrought figurative language that resembles poetry in its density and musicality, yet with no semblance of meter or regular form. Nowadays we would call it free verse.

Hildegard brought to her songs a directness, an imagistic bravura, that does away with the boundary between dogmatic statement and rhapsodic expression. Her sentences are not concisely crafted, but their irregular flow has a rhythm of its own. Unlike the leading composers of her day, she reveled in periodic sentences spun from strings of relative clauses, participial and prepositional phrases.

Hildegard's lyrics, like her prose, are rich in allusions but sparing in quotations. As someone once said of Saint Bernard of Clairvaux, she too "spoke Bible." She was so deeply immersed in the sacred page that her language rings with echoes from the Vulgate, especially from the Psalter and the Song of Songs. Yet these are seldom more than echoes, verses recalled or paraphrased rather than quoted. Hildegard had a tenacious memory for images and ideas, but no penchant for exact citation. Non-Scriptural borrowings are rare and derive most often from the liturgy. It is notoriously hard to pin down Hildegard's sources, because she made everything she touched her own.

Yet, although hers was a character of exceptionally strong will and individuality, our poet made no use of the first person singular. The *Symphonia* is poetry of public worship; no matter how distinctive the idiom, its content is monumentally objective, almost impersonal.

Hildegard's diction has acquired a reputation for difficulty, but her language is not at all precious or studied. The problem is that her basic vocabulary—like that of the Provençal troubadours—was quite small, and she relied heavily on certain polyvalent key words. *Virtus* is virtue, power, grace, divine emanation; the *virtutes* are moral qualities, but also an order of angels and a choir of celestial maidens who figure in Hildegard's *Ordo*. *Viriditas*, literally "verdure," evokes all the resilience and vitality of nature and its source, the Holy Spirit. Words such as *radix* and *materia* almost always have a metaphysical sense; the literal meanings of "root" and "matter," or "matrix" (womb), suggest something very like what Paul Tillich named the "ground of being." *Instrumentum* and *ornamentum* stand broadly for utility and beauty, but beauty of the imperishable kind that Yeats called the artifice of eternity. *Peregrinatio*, the classical word for "travel," has a distinctive medieval sense that combines the negative connotation of "exile" with the positive concept of "pilgrimage."

Among the more salient features of Hildegard's style is her fondness for the grand gesture. No fewer than fifty of her songs, or about two thirds, begin with a solemn apostrophe: "O virga ac diadema" ("O branch and diadem"), "O victoriosissimi triumphatores" ("O most victorious conquerors"), "O felix apparicio" ("O happy apparition"). Here we can detect some influence from the great "O" antiphons of Advent, which are among the most exalted

seasonal compositions in the liturgy. Hildegard had a corresponding zeal for superlatives and sudden outbursts. The ecstatic "O"
can surface even in the middle of a line or strophe.

The feature for which Hildegard's poetry is best known is its
unusual imagery, which can seem outlandish insofar as it reflects
her compressed, synesthetic mode of perception. It is not simply

Saint Bernard of Clairvaux. The eye of
God speaks to Bernard and reminds
him that he is not omniscient
(only God can be).

that Hildegard used multiple metaphors to characterize a single
object; this is a common trait of devotional writing. We find it, for
instance, in Saint Bernard's famous sermon on the Name of Jesus.
Beginning with his metaphor of the holy name as light, Bernard
runs quickly through the images of food, oil, salt, honey, music,
and medicine before circling back to the light of dawn. But confu-

sion cannot arise because all these metaphors are logically and grammatically discrete; they are not mingled but juxtaposed. The resultant sensual richness contributes to an impression of spiritual and intellectual richness, but each element is singled out for separate analysis. Contrast the very different use of metaphor in Hildegard's responsory for the patriarchs and prophets:

> *O vos felices radices*
> *cum quibus opus miraculorum*
> *et non opus criminum*
> *per torrens iter*
> *perspicue umbre*
> *plantatum est.*

> O you fortunate roots
> with which the work of miracles
> and not the work of crimes
> was planted
> through a rushing course
> of transparent shadow.

The images in these lines mix freely and unself-consciously. Roots evoke the lineage of Christ, and bright shadow, the chiaroscuro of prophetic vision. But although the two images are grammatically linked, their unity is intuitive rather than logical; the reader who sets out to construct a single coherent picture can go badly astray. As in Bernard's sermon, the signs refer vertically to the signified and not horizontally to each other. Yet where Bernard's syntax discriminates, Hildegard's unites, creating possibilities both for confusion and for extraordinary richness. Each image is an independent unit of meaning, a motif, that can appear in a variety of contexts. Just as she combined many short, formulaic musical phrases to spin a long melody, Hildegard could vary and recombine units of textual meaning to create unexpected wholes.

*Adoration of the Magi. Illumination from a German
Gospel lectionary, circa 1225.*

Given that the *Symphonia* lyrics were meant to be sung, it may seem perverse to consider their sonority as purely verbal constructs. But even from this perspective, some of them have a pronounced musicality, based on assonance, alliteration, *annominatio* (which links etymologically related words), and occasional rhyme.

Most writers of artistic prose were careful to follow the rules of *cursus,* or cadence, which medieval rhetoricians had adapted from antiquity. According to this convention, every sentence or important clause had to end in one of four patterns of stressed and unstressed syllables as follows:

planus—u u–u

tardus—u u–u u

velox—u u u u–u

dispondaicus—u u u–u

A review of the *Symphonia* lyrics shows that exactly two thirds end with some form of cursus. Cursus rhythms are natural to the structure of Latin, and if Hildegard had been following the rules systematically, there would no doubt be fewer exceptions. Nevertheless, her strong predilection for these cadences marks the lyrics as less "raw" than has sometimes been argued.

Often conventional in her subjects, Hildegard was wholly original in her treatment and style. Her poems, even apart from their musical settings, leave an indelible impression of freshness and power. What she lacked in fluency, Hildegard made up for in sheer immediacy. Not words but images formed her native idiom, and in her lyrics these images can leap out of their verbal wrappings to assault the mind with all the force and inevitability of a Jungian dream. Startling at first, even incoherent, they slowly or suddenly explode into sense, revealing the lineaments of a pattern that—if one is a twelfth-century Christian—one has always known.

"O virga ac diadema" ("Praise for the Mother")
Sequence for the Virgin

1a. *O virga ac diadema*
    purpure regis,
    que es in clausura tua
    sicut lorica:

1b. *Tu frondens floruisti*
    in alia vicissitudine
    quam Adam omne genus humanum
    produceret.

2a. *Ave, ave, de tuo ventre*
    alia vita processit
    qua Adam filios suos
    denudaverat.

2b. *O flos, tu non germinasti de rore*
    nec de guttis pluvie,
    nec aer desuper to volavit,
    sed divina claritas
    in nobilissima virga te produxit.

3a. *O virga, floriditatem tuam*
    Deus in prima die
    creature sue previderat.

3b. *Et te Verbo suo*
    auream materiam,
    o laudabilis Virgo, fecit.

4a. *O quam magnum est*
    in viribus suis latus viri,
    de quo Deus forman mulieris produxit,
    quam fecit speculum
    omnis ornamenti sui

et amplexionem
omnis creature sue.

4b. *Inde concinunt celestia organa*
    et miratur omnis terra,
    o laudabilis Maria,
    quia Deus te valde amavit.

5a. *O quam valde plangendum et lugendum est*
    quod tristicia in crimine
    per consilium serpentis
    in mulierem fluxit.

5b. *Nam ipsa mulier*
    quam Deus matrem omnium posuit
    viscera sua
    cum vulneribus ignorantie decerpsit,
    et plenum dolorem
    generi suo protulit.

6a. *Sed, o aurora,*
    de ventre tuo
    novus sol processit,
    qui omnia crimina Eve abstersit
    et maiorem benedictionem per to protulit
    quam Eva hominibus nocuisset.

6b. *Unde, o Salvatrix,*
    que novum lumen
    humano generi protulisti:
    collige membra Filii tui
    ad celestem armoniam.

1a. O branch and diadem
    of the king's purple,
    strong in your enclosure
    like a breastplate:

1b. Burgeoning, you blossomed
after another fashion
than Adam gave rise
to the whole human race.

2a. Hail, hail! from your womb
came another life
of which Adam
had stripped his sons.

2b. O flower, you did not spring from the dew
nor from drops of rain,
nor did the air sweep over you,
but the divine radiance
brought you forth on a most noble branch.

3a. O branch, God had foreseen your flowering
on the first day
of His creation.

3b. And He made you for His Word
as a golden matrix,
O praiseworthy Virgin.

4a. O how great
in its powers is the side of man
from which God brought forth the form of woman,
which He made the mirror
of all His beauty
and the embrace
of His whole creation.

4b. Thence celestial voices chime in harmony
and the whole earth marvels,
O praiseworthy Mary,
for God has greatly loved you.

The Life and Music of Hildegard von Bingen

A walkway in a twelfth-century cloister, Bad Reichenhall, Germany. One of the definitions of cloister *is "A covered passage on the side of a court usually having one side walled and the other an open arcade or colonnade." It would have been in a cloister such as this where three of Hildegard's nuns claimed to have seen her spirit walk, chanting "Praise for the Mother."*

5a. O how greatly we must lament and mourn
because sadness flowed in guilt
through the serpent's counsel
into woman.

5b. For the very woman
whom God made to be mother of all
plucked at her womb
with the wombs of ignorance
and brought forth consummate pain
for her kind.

6a. But, O dawn,
from your womb
a new sun has come forth,
which has cleansed all the guilt of Eve
and through you brought a blessing greater
than the harm Eve did to mankind.

6b. Hence, O saving Lady,
you who bore the new light
for humankind:
gather the members of your Son
into celestial harmony.

When inquisitors came to Bingen after Hildegard's death to
seek witnesses for her canonization, they found three nuns who
swore they had seen their mistress illuminated by the Holy Spirit
as she walked through the cloister, chanting the above sequence.
Hildegard had reason to be pleased with it, for it ranks with the
finest of her work. The sequence falls logically into three parts,
each composed of two strophic pairs, with a parallelism between
the first and third parts. In 1b through 2b, Mary's childbearing is
contrasted with natural generation, in particular with Adam's,
while in 5a through 6a, Mary is compared with Eve, and the no-
tion of fortunate fall is evoked. The initial salutation to a queenly

figure (1a) is balanced by a final prayer to the Virgin as *salvatrix*, or feminine savior (6b). In the central section, strophes 3 and 4, Hildegard returns to her theme of Mary as God's foreordained bride. The striking exclamation of 4a conflates Mary and Eve; it is the "form of woman" which God has blessed in the one and the other, making it the centerpiece of the cosmos. *Organa* in 4b could refer in Hildegard's period either to musical instruments or to harmonized chant.

"Sed diabolus" ("Only the Devil Laughed")
Psalm antiphon for the 11,000 virgins

> Sed diabolus in invidia sua
> istud irrisit,
> qua nullum opus Dei
> intactum dimisit.

> Only the devil laughed
> honor to scorn:
> in his envy he left
> no work of God untouched.

A fresco from 1380, in a cross vault, depicting Saint Ursula. The story of Ursula appears to have been mostly a legend, gaining enormous popularity in the twelfth century when, not coincidentally, women such as Hildegard were gaining power in Church affairs.

The Life and Music of Hildegard von Bingen

■ ■

The Apotheosis of Saint Ursula, *by Vittore Carpaccio (ca. 1460–*
1525/26). Ursula, to avoid an unwanted marriage, departed from
Britain in the company of her maidens, reputed to number eleven
thousand. In Cologne, Germany, the group was slaughtered by
Huns because of their faith, and so became virgin martyrs.

Like "Unde quocumque" and "Deus enim rorem" (see below), "Sed diabolus" is one of eight antiphons labeled *In matutinis laudibus* ("for matins") in the Dendermonde codex and *Laudes* ("lauds" or "praises") in the Riesenkodex. They are musically distinct, each with its own psalm differentia, but textually they make up a single narrative. The exact liturgical setting of the pieces remains a puzzle; perhaps matins and lauds were sung consecutively as one service.

The antiphons relate Ursula's story from her initial call to a point just before her martyrdom. Two themes are singled out for emphasis: public response to the virgins' enterprise and the role of men in their company. Having led her own band of virgins to the Rupertsberg, in the face of strong opposition as well as support, Hildegard clearly sympathized with Ursula's venture. There is something Ursuline about her recollections of her own move to the new foundation: "by the archbishop's permission, with a vast escort of our kinsfolk and of other men, in reverence of God we came to this place. Then the ancient deceiver put me to the ordeal of great mockery, in that many people said: '. . . Surely this will come to nothing!'" In the same way Ursula's virgins are seen to be famous in the sight of "all peoples" and accompanied by an honorable escort, until the devil through his envy stirs up mockery.

Four of the eight antiphons justify the virgins' male companionship. Women, as the composer firmly believed, needed men to protect and care for them even—or especially—if they had chosen the life of virginity. In a Christmas sermon, she once preached that the Mother of God herself was wedded for the sake of humility: "If Mary had had no one to care for her, pride would easily have snatched her, as if she had not needed a husband to provide for her."

"O Euchari in leta via" ("Vision")
Sequence for Saint Eucharius

1a. *O Euchari,*
  in leta via ambulasti
  ubi cum Filio Dei mansisti,
  illum tangendo
  et miracula eius que fecit videndo.

1b. *Tu eum perfecte amasti*
  cum sodales tui exterriti erant,
  pro eo quod homines erant,
  nec possibilitatem habebant
  bona perfecte intueri.

2a. *Tu autem in ardenti amore plene caritatis*
  illum amplexus es,
  cum manipulos preceptorum eius
  ad te collegisti.

2b. *O Euchari,*
  valde beatus fuisti
  cum Verbum Dei te in igne columbe imbuit,
  ubi tu quasi aurora illuminatus es,
  et sic fundamentum ecclesie
  edificasti.

3a. *Et in pectore tuo*
  choruscat dies
  in quo tria tabernacula
  supra marmoream columpnam stant
  in civitate Dei.

3b. *Per os tuum Ecclesia ruminat*
  vetus et novum vinum,
  videlicet poculum sanctitatis.

4a. *Sed et in tua doctrina*
    Ecclesia effecta est racionalis,
    ita quod supra montes clamavit
    ut colles et ligna se declinarent
    ac mamillas illius sugerent.

4b. *Nunc in tua clara voce*
    Filium Dei ora pro hac turba,
    ne in cerimoniis Dei deficiat,
    sed ut vivens holocaustum
    ante altare Dei fiat.

1a. O Eucharius,
    you walked in a joyful path
    when you stayed with the Son of God,
    touching Him
    and seeing the miracles He did.

1b. You loved him perfectly
    when your companions were terrified,
    because they were human
    and had no power
    to gaze fully on the good.

2a. But you embraced Him
    in the ardent love of perfect charity
    when you gathered to yourself
    the sheaves of His commandments.

2b. O Eucharius,
    you were greatly blessed
    when the Word of God steeped you
    in the fire of the dove,
    where you were illumined like the dawn,
    and thus you built
    the foundation of a church.

The Life and Music of Hildegard von Bingen

3a. And in your breast
    sparkles the daylight
    in which three tabernacles
    stand on a marble column
    in the city of God.

3b. Through your mouth the Church savors
    old and new wine,
    the chalice of holiness.

4a. But in your teaching
    the Church was made rational
    so that she cried out above the mountains,
    that the hills and the woods might bow
    and suck her breasts.

4b. Now in your clear voice
    pray the Son of God for this flock,
    that it may not fail in the ceremonies of God,
    but become a living sacrifice
    before God's altar.

A narrative sequence recalling the phases of Eucharius's life. As a young man he traveled with Christ (1a), and after the baptism of fire on Pentecost, he went to evangelize Trier and founded a church there (2b). The *sodales* of 1b are his missionary companions, Valerius and Maternus, portrayed as men of goodwill but insufficient courage in the face of martyrdom. Eucharius himself survived stoning by paralyzing his tormentors with a prayer; after they were converted, he released them. His fearful companions' inability to "gaze fully on the good" leads toward an evocation of the transfigured Christ, from whom the three chosen apostles had to avert their eyes. Peter nonetheless offered to build three tabernacles in the unearthly light (Matthew 17:4); in 3a Hildegard has transposed them from Mount Tabor into the City of God, where the saint now enjoys a lasting vision of Christ in glory. Strophes

3b and 4a recall his preaching: the "old and new wine" of Christ's parable (Matthew 9:17) stand for the Old and New Testaments, though the eucharistic chalice is also called to mind. In 4a the missionary merges with the powerful figure of Mother Church, who nurses the world with the milk of doctrine, inverting the messianic promise of Isaiah 60:16.

■ ■

Portrait of Saint Matthew from a German Gospel,
circa 1200–1220.

The Life and Music of Hildegard von Bingen

"O viridissima virga" ("Song to the Mother")
Free song to the Virgin

1. *O viridissima virga, ave,*
   que in ventoso flabro sciscitationis
   sanctorum prodisti.

2. *Cum venit tempus*
   quod tu floruisti in ramis tuis,
   ave, ave fuit tibi,
   quia calor solis in te sudavit
   sicut odor balsami.

3. *Nam in te floruit pulcher flos*
   qui odorem dedit
   omnibus aromatibus
   que arida erant.

4. *Et illa apparuerunt omnia*
   in viriditate plena.

5. *Unde celi dederunt rorem super gramen*
   et omnis terra leta facta est,
   quoniam viscera ipsius frumentum protulerunt
   et quoniam volucres celi
   nidos in ipsa habuerunt.

6. *Deinde facta est esca hominibus*
   et gaudium magnum epulantium.
   Unde, o suavis Virgo,
   in te non deficit ullum gaudium.

7. *Hec omnia Eva contempsit.*

8. *Nunc autem laus sit Altissimo.*

1. Hail, O greenest branch,
   you who came forth in the windy blast
   of the questioning of saints.

2. When the time came
   that you blossomed in your branches—
   hail, hail was [the word] to you!
   for the warmth of the sun distilled in you
   a fragrance like balsam.

3. For in you blossomed the beautiful flower
   that gave fragrance
   to all the spices
   dry though they were.

4. And they all appeared
   in full verdure.

5. Hence the heavens dropped dew upon the grass
   and the whole earth was made glad,
   because her womb brought forth wheat,
   and the birds of heaven
   made their nests in it.

6. Then a meal was prepared for humanity,
   and great joy for the banqueters.
   Hence, O sweet Virgin,
   in you no joy is lacking.

7. Eve despised all these things.

8. Now, however,
   praise be to the Most High.

A favorite motif in manuscript paintings and cathedral windows is the Tree of Jesse, which represents the genealogy of Christ. As the father of David lies sleeping, the Messiah's family tree is seen to rise from his loins, with prophets and ancestors of Christ seated on the several branches and pointing to Mary enthroned in the crown. The first stanza of this song is an analogous verbal icon. In the remainder of the lyric, the tree image is developed with skill and subtlety, enriched by a plethora of biblical echoes. The me-

dieval singer or listener would no doubt recall the rich spices in the
Song of Songs, Christ's parable of the green tree and the dry tree
(Luke 23:31), the Advent antiphon beseeching dew from the
heavens (Isaiah 45:8), and the great tree of the Kingdom in which
the birds of the air build their nests (Matthew 13:32). The "meal"
of wheat bread is of course the Eucharist, which is also the heavenly wedding feast. In *Scivias* II.6.26 Hildegard explained that only
wheat is used for the sacramental bread, because it is a dry and pure
grain, free from pith as Mary was free from "the pith of man."

"Unde quocumque" ("Wherever")
Psalm antiphon for the 11,000 virgins

Unde quocumque venientes
perrexerunt,
velut cum gaudio celestis paradisi
suscepte sunt,
quia in religione morum
honorifice apparuerunt.

Hence, wherever they arrived,
they were welcomed
as with the joy of
celestial paradise,
because in the religious life
they appeared full of honor.

See "Sed diabolus," page 81.

"O frondens virga" ("For the Virgin")
Psalm antiphon for the Virgin

O frondens virga,
in tua nobilitate stans
sicut aurora procedit:

nunc gaude et letare
et nos debiles dignare
a mala consuetudine liberare
atque manum tuam porrige
ad erigendum nos.

O leafy branch,
standing in your nobility
as the dawn breaks forth:
now rejoice and be glad
and deign to set us frail ones
free from evil habits
and stretch forth your hand
to lift us up.

This antiphon (with "Laus Trinitati") is one of only two pieces that appear in the earlier Dendermonde manuscript but not in the Riesenkodex. Peter Dronke has suggested that Hildegard chose to exclude them on poetic grounds. "O frondens virga" is an almost unadorned prayer of a sort rare in the *Symphonia*. But note the triple rhyme in lines 4–6.

"O quam mirabilis" ("For the Creator")
Votive antiphon

O quam mirabilis est
prescientia divini pectoris
que prescivit omnem creaturam.
Nam cum Deus inspexit
faciem hominis quem formavit,
omnia opera sua
in eadem forma hominis
integra aspexit.
O quam mirabilis est inspiratio
que hominem sic suscitavit.

The Life and Music of Hildegard von Bingen

Relief, circa 1130, over the portal of an abbey in Andlau-bei-Barr, Germany, depicting God, Peter, and Paul.

O how marvelous is
the foreknowledge of the divine heart
that foreknew all creation.
For when God looked
on the face of the man whom He formed,
He saw all his works whole
in that same human form.
O how marvelous is the inspiration
that in this way roused man to life.

Hildegard dwelt frequently and joyfully on the theme of predestination, which for her meant the eternal existence of the world in the mind of God before it emerged in time, when the Father uttered the Word. Man, the microcosm, occupies a central place in the newborn cosmos, as he is God's image and consummate work.

In him the angelic and material creations meet, and with the coming of the God-man and the descent of the Holy Spirit, all creation is destined to attain union with the Creator through the redeemed human race. In the antiphon, God looks at the newly created Adam and affirms his sublime potential.

"Deus enim rorem" ("This Honorable Fame")
Psalm antiphon for the 11,000 virgins

Deus enim rorem in illas misit,
de quo multiplex fama crevit,
ita quod omnes populi
ex hac honorabili fama
velut cibum gustabant.

For God sent upon them a dew
from which manifold fame sprang up,
so that all peoples
tasted of this honorable fame
like a food.

See "Sed diabolus," page 81.

"Laus Trinitati" ("For the Trinity")
Votive antiphon

Laus Trinitati
que sonus et vita
ac creatrix omnium
in vita ipsorum est,
et que laus angelice turbe
et mirus splendor archanorum,
que hominibus ignota sunt, est,
et que in omnibus vita est.

The Life and Music of Hildegard von Bingen

Praise to the Trinity,
which is sound and life
and creatrix of all beings
in their life.
It is the praise of the angelic host
and the wondrous splendor of arcane mysteries
unknown to humankind:
the Trinity is the life in all.

One of the composer's least effective lyrics, redundant and grammatically awkward. Its themes are more successfully treated in another votive antiphon, "O gloriosissimi lux vivens angeli" ("O most glorious living-light angels").

The medieval heaven, like society on earth as theorists conceived it, followed strict principles of decorum and order. After God the Father, Christ the King, and Mary the Queen came the ranks of the blessed, all in their proper stations: first the nine orders of angels, then the saints in their several categories—patriarchs and prophets, apostles, martyrs, confessors or holy bishops, virgins, widows, and innocents.

Angels, for Hildegard, signified the perfection of praise. As pure mirrors of the eternal light, they provide images of the fulfillment that every soul desires.

"O vas nobile" ("The Chalice")
From an irregular sequence for Saint Rupert

O vas nobile,
quod non est pollutum
nec devoratum
in saltatione antique spelunce,
et quod non est maceratum
in vulneribus antiqui perditoris:

Saint Rupert. From an altarpiece in Saint Peter's Church,
Salzburg, Austria, by G. Staber, circa 1500.

Your body's a chalice,
its wine never drained
in the ancient cave dance.
The ancient foe
could not ravish
or scar your flesh.

On May 1, 1152, Hildegard's new monastic church at the Rupertsberg was consecrated to the Mother of God as well as Saints Philip and James, Martin and Rupert. The sequence for Saint Rupert, "O Ierusalem" ("O Jerusalem"), the longest and most carefully crafted in the *Symphonia*, might have been composed for that festive occasion. "O vas nobile" is a strophe from that sequence, which commemorates not only Rupert but the whole communion of saints, the living stones in celestial Jerusalem, among whom the abbess and her nuns aspired to shine.

The strophe praises Rupert's virginity; his "vessel," or body, remains undefiled, untouched by Satan, and like Mary he "has no stain" (Song of Songs 4:7). The tantalizing "dance of the ancient cave" remains unexplained, but as Peter Dronke has suggested, Hildegard seems to be juxtaposing an orgiastic pagan rite with the divine music and dance of the angels.

"Karitas habundat" ("Divine Love")
Psalm antiphon

Karitas
habundat in omnia,
de imis excellentissima
super sidera
atque amantissima
in omnia,
quia summo regi osculum pacis
dedit.

Charity
abounds toward all,
most exalted from the depths
above the stars,
and most loving
toward all,
for she has given
the supreme King the kiss of peace.

Lady Love, or Charity, occupied a central place in Hildegard's visionary world. In the great cosmic vision that opens her last book, *On the Activity of God,* Caritas proclaims herself identical to the Trinity, but also to the *anima mundi,* or world soul: "I am the supreme and fiery force who kindled every living spark, and I breathed forth no deadly thing. . . . And I am the fiery life of the essence of God: I flame above the beauty of the fields; I shine in the waters; I burn in the sun, the moon, and the stars." Sometimes she seems equivalent to Wisdom, and at other times to the Holy Spirit; in both *Symphonia* manuscripts, this antiphon directly follows "Spiritus sanctus vivificans vita" ("The Holy Spirit is a life-giving life"). Here Caritas is in heaven what the Virgin Mary is on earth, the queen consort of God—that divinely feminine spirit whom no effort of doctrine could ever quite exclude from His throne.

"Hodie aperuit" ("The Flower Gleams")
Psalm antiphon for the Virgin

Hodie aperuit nobis
clausa porta
quod serpens in muliere suffocavit,
unde lucet in aurora
flos de Virgine Maria.

The Life and Music of Hildegard von Bingen

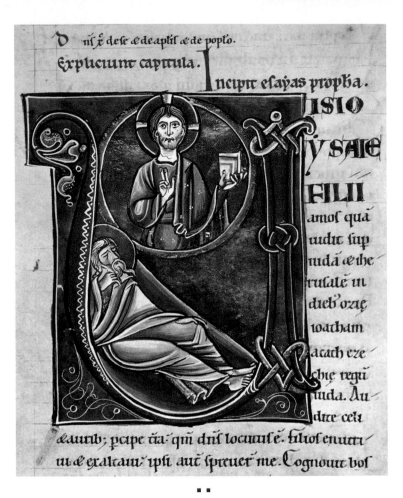

Illustration of Isaiah's vision. From the Bible of Saint Sulpice of Bourges, the second half of the twelfth century.

Today a closed gate
has opened to us the door
the serpent slammed on a woman:
the flower of the maiden Mary
gleams in the dawn.

VISION

For medieval students of the Bible, the closed gate of the temple in Ezekiel's vision was a sign of Mary's perpetual virginity, "for the Lord, the God of Israel, has entered by it; therefore it shall remain shut. Only the prince may sit in it" (Ezekiel 44:2–3). In this antiphon, the closed gate, which is Mary's womb, opens paradise; and through its portals the faithful can glimpse the sunrise of a new creation lighting its first vernal blossom. The image is crisp and startling, though muted by the indefinite *quod* of line 3. The initial *hodie* strikes a note of liturgical immediacy that would be proper to a specific feast, such as the Annunciation or Christmas.

"Cum erubuerint" ("From This Wicked Fall")
Psalm antiphon for the Virgin

Cum erubuerint
infelices in progenie sua,
procedentes in peregrinatione casus,
tunc tu clamas clara voce,
hoc modo homines elevans
de isto malicioso
casu.

While the unhappy ones were blushing
at their offspring
walking in the exile of the fall,
then you cry out with a clear voice,
in this way lifting humanity
from this wicked
fall.

Hildegard expresses the opposing roles of woman in salvation history, embodied in the figures of Eve and Mary, in a remembrance of the Fall set against the sound of Mary's redeeming voice,

The Life and Music of Hildegard von Bingen

Relief, circa 1130, in an abbey in Andlau-bei-Barr, Germany, showing the story of the Fall: Eve emerges from Adam's rib; God warns Adam and Eve of the Tree of Knowledge; Adam and Eve under the Tree of Knowledge with the serpent; an angel expels Adam and Eve from paradise, and they know their own nakedness; Adam and Eve after the expulsion.

which she credits with the power to transform human fate. There is a striking tense change from the perfect subjunctive to the present in line 4. The *infelices* ("unhappy ones") are Adam and Eve.

"O vivens fons" ("Living Fountain")
From Ordo virtutum

O vivens fons, quam magna est suavitas tua,
qui faciem istorum in te non amisisti,
sed acute previdisti
quomodo eos de angelico casu abstraheres
qui se estimabant illud habere

quod non licet sic stare;
unde gaude, filia Syon,
quia Deus tibi multos reddit
quos serpens de te abscidere voluit,
qui nunc in maiori luce fulgent
quam prius illorum causa fuisset.

Living fountain, how great is your sweetness:
you did not reject the gaze of these upon you—
no, acutely you foresaw
how you could avert them from a fall as of the angels,
they who thought they possessed a power
which cannot lawfully subsist like that.
Rejoice then, daughter of Jerusalem,
for God is giving you back many
whom the serpent wanted to sunder from you,
who now gleam in a greater brightness
than would have been their lot before.

The thought of these syntactically difficult lines, from the close of scene iii of the *Ordo virtutum*, seems to be that God has

not rejected the gaze of sinners, but has foreseen (through the re-
demptive process) how to divert them from a fall such as the angels
had: the angels who fell thought that they possessed a thing (divine
sovereignty) that cannot lawfully subsist thus (among created
things).

■ ■

OPPOSITE: *A present-day radio and television production of
Hildegard's morality play* Ordo virtutum *by Westdeutscher
Rundfunk Köln (WDR) performed in May 1982 in
Germany. A tapestry of one of Hildegard's visions,*
The Redeemer, *hangs in the background.*

VISION

*Portrait of Saint Matthew from a German
Gospel, ca. 1200–1220.*

BIBLIOGRAPHICAL NOTE

The account of Hildegard's life and works given here is based on Sabina Flanagan, *Hildegard of Bingen, 1098–1179: A Visionary Life* (London and New York: Routledge, 1989); Barbara Newman, *Sister of Wisdom: St. Hildegard's Theology of the Feminine* (Berkeley and Los Angeles: University of California Press, 1987); Saint Hildegard of Bingen, *Symphonia: A Critical Edition of the* Symphonia armonie celestium revelationum (*Symphony of the Harmony of Celestial Revelations*), intro., trans., and commentary by Barbara Newman (Ithaca and London: Cornell University Press, 1988); and Fiona Bowie and Oliver Davies, eds., *Hildegard of Bingen: Mystical Writings* (New York: Crossroad, 1993).

On medieval spirituality from a woman's perspective, see Frances Beer, *Women and Mystical Experience in the Middle Ages* (Woodbridge: The Boydell Press, 1992); Peter Dronke, *Women Writers of the Middle Ages: A Critical Study of Texts from Perpetua (+ 203) to Marguerite Porete (+ 1310)* (Cambridge: Cambridge University Press, 1984); and Elizabeth Petroff, ed., *Medieval Women's Visionary Literature* (New York: Oxford University Press, 1986).

Many of Hildegard's writings have been translated into English. They include *Hildegard of Bingen: Scivias*, trans. Columba Hart and Jane Bishop (New York: Paulist Press, 1990); *Scivias*, trans. Bruce Hozeski (Santa Fe: Bear & Co., 1986); *Hildegard of Bingen: The Book of the Rewards of Life*, trans. Bruce W. Hozeski (New York: Garland, 1994); *Hildegard of Bingen's "Book of Divine Works" with Letters and Songs*, ed. Matthew Fox (Santa Fe: Bear & Co., 1987); and *The Letters of Hildegard of Bingen*, vol. 1, trans. Joseph L. Baird and Radd K. Ehrman (New York: Oxford

University Press, 1994). Bowie and Davies's *Hildegard of Bingen: Mystical Writings* contains selections from *Scivias*, the *Liber vitae meritorum*, *De operatione Dei*, *Causae et curae*, and Hildegard's songs and letters. Matthew Fox, *Illuminations of Hildegard of Bingen* (Santa Fe: Bear & Co., 1985), reproduces twenty-three illuminations from *Scivias*, and two from *De operatione Dei*.

Newman's edition of Hildegard's *Symphonia* includes all the original Latin texts of the liturgical cycle, as well as both literal prose translations and verse renditions of the songs. Among the available performance editions of portions of the *Symphonia* are Christopher Page, ed., *Abbess Hildegard of Bingen: Sequences and Hymns* (Devon: Antico, 1983), and three transcriptions by Pozzi Escot: *Three Antiphons* (Bryn Mawr, Pa.: Hildegard Publishing Company, 1990); *Sequentia de sancto Maximino: Columba aspexit* (Bryn Mawr, Pa.: Hildegard Publishing Company, 1992); and *The Ursula Antiphons* (Bryn Mawr, Pa.: Hildegard Publishing Company, 1994). The Latin text of the *Ordo virtutum* may be found in Peter Dronke, *Poetic Individuality in the Middle Ages: New Departures in Poetry, 1000–1150* (Oxford: Clarendon Press, 1970); an English translation, by Peter Dronke, in the record liner for *Hildegard von Bingen: Ordo virtutum*, recorded by Sequentia (Harmonia mundi 20395/96); and a performance edition in Audrey Davidson, ed., *The "Ordo virtutum" of Hildegard of Bingen* (Kalamazoo: Medieval Institute Publications, 1985).

For further reading, the bibliographies in Flanagan, Bowie and Davies, Newman's *Symphonia*, and *The Letters* are recommended.

Discographies appear in Newman's *Symphonia*, and in Bowie and Davies.

INDEX

Index

The publisher gratefully acknowledges the following:

The translation of quotes by Guibert of Gembloux on pages three and thirty-five are from *Sister of Wisdom: St. Hildegard's Theology of the Feminine*, Barbara Newman. Copyright © 1987, The Regents of the University of California. By permission of the University of California Press.

The translation of quotes by Hildegard von Bingen appearing on page thirty-two are from *Hildegard of Bingen: Mystical Writings*, edited and introduced by Fiona Bowie and Oliver Davies, with new translations by Robert Carver. Translation copyright © Robert Carver 1990. Reprinted by permission of The CROSSROADS Publishing Co., New York.

The material by Matthew Fox in chapter two is reprinted from *Illuminations of Hildegard of Bingen*, commentary by Matthew Fox. Copyright © 1985, Bear & Co., Inc., P.O. Box 2860, Sante Fe, New Mexico 87504.

The material by Barbara Newman in chapter three is reprinted from St. Hildegard of Bingen: *Symphonia: A Critical Edition of the Symphonia armonie celestium revelationum*. Edited and translated by Barbara Newman. Copyright © 1989 by Cornell University. Used by permission of the publisher, Cornell University Press.

The publisher thanks the organizations below:

Otto Müller Verlag, Salzburg, for permission to reproduce the art on pages: ii, 34, 39, 41, 47, 49, 51, 53, 55, 57, 59, 61 from *Wisse die Wege* by Hildegard von Bingen and the work on page 67 from *Hildegard von Bingen: Lieder* by Pudentiana Barth et al.

Dr. W. Bahnmüller Bildverlag, München, for permission to reproduce the art on pages: 8, 25, 33, 62, 64, 78–79, 81, 92, 95, 100–101.

The Granger Collection, New York, for permission to reproduce the art on pages: 2, 7, 10, 23, 24, 30, 71, 73, 87, 104.

Giraudon/Art Resource, New York, for permission to reproduce the art on pages: 11, 98.

Erich Lessing/Art Resource, New York, for permission to reproduce the art on pages: 5, 82.

The Pierpont Morgan Library/Art Resource, New York, for permission to reproduce the art on page 16.

Scala/Art Resource, New York, for permission to reproduce the art on pages: 27, 43, 45.

Superstock, New York, for permission to reproduce art on page 20.

A. Engelhardt-Rotthaus for permission to reproduce the art on pages 12–13 from *Hildegard von Bingen*, Friedrich Rudolf Engelhardt, Verlag A. Engelhardt, Bingen, 1979.

Bear & Co., Inc., Sante Fe, New Mexico, for permission to reproduce the art on pages 28–29 from *Illuminations of Hildegard von Bingen*, by Matthew Fox. Copyright 1985 Bear & Co., Inc., P. O. Box 2860, Santa Fe, New Mexico, 87504

Westdeutscher Rundfunk (WDR), Köln, for permission to reproduce the art on page 103.